Sheila E. Harvey,
See Page 49

1998

Those Three Little Words

Edited by

Heather Killingray

First published in Great Britain in 1998 by
POETRY NOW
1-2 Wainman Road, Woodston,
Peterborough, PE2 7BU
Telephone (01733) 230746
Fax (01733) 230751

HB ISBN 1 86188 633 0
SB ISBN 1 86188 628 4

FOREWORD

Although we are a nation of poetry writers we are accused of not reading poetry and not buying poetry books: after many years of listening to the incessant gripes of poetry publishers, I can only assume that the books they publish, in general, are books that most people do not want to read.

Poetry should not be obscure, introverted, and as cryptic as a crossword puzzle: it is the poet's duty to reach out and embrace the world.

The world owes the poet nothing and we should not be expected to dig and delve into a rambling discourse searching for some inner meaning.

The reason we write poetry (and almost all of us do) is because we want to communicate: an ideal; an idea; or a specific feeling. Poetry is as essential in communication, as a letter; a radio; a telephone, and the main criteria for selecting the poems in this anthology is very simple: they communicate.

With each relationship comes trials and tribulations. Some relationships last five minutes, others are destined for eternity.

Love holds many emotions such as, fear, compassion, hate, completeness, each of which are individual to their owner.

Those Three Little Words is an anthology dedicated to the trials and errors of love. Some people have been lucky, others have been hurt. Each poet has something to express about their experiences and thoughts.

CONTENTS

To Chris

When the pain is strong
And the night is long
Be brave, my friend

When you feel so weak
You just want to weep
Be strong, my friend

Whilst you are so low
You need to know
You will be alright
Your future is bright

Soon the doubts will go
And you will know
You are well, my friend

Lin MacDonald

LOVE TO TREASURE

Romance is in the air you see
love to feel eternally.
Happiness radiates afar
those sparkling eyes and twinkling star.

Flowers bloom many joys to share
kindness giving warmth and care.
Those candle-lights and meal delight
red roses too, a pleasing sight.

This gift of love for one and all
cherish then that babe so small.
Treasure moments throughout your life
with love we all can conquer strife.

Such love to feel where're we go
peace and laughter ever flow.
Much gentleness in all we do
golden days when this sun shines through.

Margaret Jackson

MY TRUE LOVE
(Look In My Heart)

Brighter than sunlight the eyes of my true love,
Paler than moonlight the tone of her skin,
Fragrant as springtime the scent of her near me,
Look in my heart, you will find her within.

Sweeter than honey the kiss of my true love,
Brighter than summer her long golden hair,
Smoother than silk the caress of her fingers,
Look in my heart, you will find her in there.

Sweeter than bird-song the voice of my true love,
Warmer than sunshine the smile on her face,
Empty my arms now she's no longer with me,
Look in my heart, you will find her in place.

Gone to a new life in Heaven my true love,
Gone with the sound of the funeral bells,
Gone is her soul but her spirit stays with me,
Look in my heart, you will find where she dwells.

David R Williams

LOVE HURTS

Love! Love is such a wonderful thing
We think of the pleasures that love can bring
The light in our eyes when we see our love's face
That wonderful feeling that nought can efface.

But love can be such a hurtful thing
Some try to make shackles out of a ring.
By trying to change our loved one's ways
We can squabble and grumble all our days.

Although we know we are one at heart
We have our own lives to lead, sometimes apart.
We must learn and remember all else above
If love didn't hurt it wouldn't be love.

J Mortimer

SEPTEMBER FRUITS

Blood red, lip red juice,
dog days
distilled, holding promise
come of age,
this auspicious Autumn date
bursts with Summer's fire,
your September sun.
Heady wine,
intoxicates the months . . .
the years
still to come,
the proof of harvest home
and with the standing sheaf
lives on
our spirit for the Springtime seed.

Shine on September sun.

Martyn Barlow

LAMENT FOR A HUSBAND

Johnnie, oh Johnnie where are you?
Johnnie where have you gone?
Oh Johnnie, Johnnie I miss you.
How can I carry on?

Johnnie, how could you leave me
After sixty-three married years?
I'm ninety years old, I'm lonely,
I hurt and I cannot shed tears.

Oh Johnnie, now you have left me
Living here all on my own.
I never thought you'd go before
Why should I be left alone?

We'd always planned I would go first.
Why did you change that plan?
You ought to be here with me,
For you were my love, my man.

Sometimes I think you are still here
I call you, but there's no reply.
My hearing is bad. I hate hearing-aids
And I'm losing the sight in my eyes.

Oh my dear husband I'm hurting.
Almost all of my spirit has gone.
Come and fetch me, I can't live without you.
Don't leave me here for too long.

Norma Langley

ST VALENTINE'S DAY DILEMMA

May
I send her a card on St Valentine's Day,
Or not?
For I've, seemingly 'given my best shot',

And failed . . .

Would she run away
in dismay,
My failure nailed - to the masthead?
Would I be forever blasted
For 'coming on too strong'?
Would, thus, to send her a card be wrong?

Should I dare
to bare
My emotions,
(Might it cause too many commotions?)

Would it be an inappropriate sign,
At the correct time?
Or the correct sign,
At the correct time?

I'll probably never know . . .

Paul Bartlett

THE PROMISE

When cold winds invade your heart,
and winter days seem dour and cold
Your spirit will remain unbroken
as love brings spring back again

When the night is dark and frightening
I'll hold you 'til the morning breaks
Your head upon my gentle shoulder
weeping away your heartache

When you're feeling sad and lonely
I'll wrap my love around your heart
I'll hold you close and let you sleep
and speak soft words to soothe and calm

When the storm-clouds gather close
and threaten to shatter our fragile love
I'll tell you how the rainbow's colours
shine down on us from heaven above

When our time draws to a close
I hope you'll remember me with love
Remember my heart, my love my arms
my smiles and words of soothing calm.

Rachel Cooper

SMITTEN

I didn't think it possible
To orbit into space
But that's just what happened
When I saw your eggy face.

Your nappy needed changing
Your hair was all on end
But still I dearly love you
Though you send me round the bend.

Louise Jutton

CLICHÉS FOR JANE

The moon seems pale and faded
The stars in darkness pine
They know there's no comparing
Their radiance with thine.

A rose in all its glory
Glistening with the dew
Is but some poor reflection
Of my true love for you.

So softly let them slumber
In shadow leave them be,
Flawed counterfeits of nature
Beside your majesty.

And as the dawn awakens
The sun begins to shine
Enlightening your countenance
O perfect Valentine!

David Farebrother

PULSE

Your dark eyes luring
Your perfume enduring
The scent of your skin on mine
The promise we've taken
The earth we have shaken
Your moments so avidly mine

And in the next morning
When sunrise comes calling
Your memory as real as before
And can I forget you
Or even regret you
When I yearn for your long moments more

Frank Samet

LOOK FOR LOVE

You may look, but do you see
My love for you that wants to be
With you forever, not just now

Show me the way, teach me how
To make you love me as I do you
With all these feelings
Could dreams come true

Long lonely days spent without you
Wondering where you are
Where you've been and what you do

Thinking day and night about you
You seem so very far
But not in mind and will never be
Look again and you will see
Someone who really loves you

So take your time now
No need for speed
Make sure you're right in mind
For I know that when you do
This burden will be freed

E Tomlin

TOGETHERNESS

I got old at twenty-three
The rain
The moon
Seasons, cherry blossoms
Usual things, never mysteries.

Under a star-studded sky
On grass, in trees
He whispered one line of poem
Heart to heart, I feel.

Evening spreads
Some misty powder
On my face.
I stretched out hands
To clasp his.
'Thirty years gone'
Whispering soon.
'Do you know
Once in thirty years back
I wished to sing a song.'
'Twenty-three add thirty'
I whispered 'An unsung evening,
Don't you see
The night light definitely
Has mystery'

Some words from a timeless zone
Hand in hand
Under a shy twilight moon.
Flickering truth
'I am not alone.'

Saleha Chowdhury

TO LOVE

Take my hand and walk with me
through the fields so
heavenly.
Cup my face within your hands,
let us go to wonderland.
Kiss my lips so warm and full,
with quickened breath there is no
lull.
Let me feel your heart beat fast,
and let us hope our love will
last.

M Rossi

MY BELOVED

Thou art my beloved
your kiss is sweeter than wine.
Your touch is soft and gentle
my heart to yours entwined.
Thou art my love for all time
for you first loved me.
And so I give myself to you
for all eternity.

Julie McKenzie

VALENTINE JO

You mean to me what life's s'posed to mean
from the first day I met you Jo
from our very first kiss to our baby bliss
we've so much around us to grow

If you make my day today
I'd stop the sky from turning grey
to climb the highest mountain or keep the rain off you
is a promise from my heart my love, which says babe, I love you

Now this special day's arrived
my darling Jo, will you be my valentine?
the love I've found inside my heart
is there to never let us part

Roses are red, violets are blue
a verse I now must do.
The grass is green and snow is white
my love for you it holds no height
to let my love fly through the sky
you'd see my love as it flew by
then you'd maybe question why
my love for you won't say goodbye.

Kevin Crow

VALENTINE'S DAY

Valentine's day is disgusting
So please don't mention that name
Lots of soppy cards and kisses
Yuck! I don't want to hear it again.

April Harding (9)

POWER OF LOVE

When two hearts
Share the same hopes
The same dreams
As each new dawn breaks
Another day begins
So love grows stronger
With each new passing dawn
As within each heart
There grows an everlasting bond
That time cannot diminish
Nor dim the fires within
When love is pure
So the power of love
In it's own magnitude
Will overcome the challenges
That life has to give
The power of love
Gives each of us
A meaning in life to live.

A W Harvey

MY LOVES

I'm sitting here and dreaming
Of the days when I was young
And everything was beautiful
And I had so much fun.

My first love he was handsome
I felt so very proud
Each time he came a-calling
He left me on a cloud.

My dreams were really shattered
When he turned out so false
I felt that I'd been battered
Without a worthy cause.

My second love was better
Charming kind and true
I'm glad that we got married
Our love seems always new.

Lilian M Smart

MY VALENTINE

On Valentine's Day,
You will be mine.
And our hearts will entwine,
A tendril of true love.
And will wrap around each other,
Sent from heaven up above.
And love will know no barrier,
Nor any half-closed door,
But will grow and will blossom,
With the tenderest feeling eternally - evermore.

Patricia Ellen Curtis

LOVE'S DREAM

To walk with you
with head held high
and hold your arm
as crowds pass by.
To eat with you
in public places
and lie all night
in your embraces.
To take your pain
and give you pleasure
would fill my cup
beyond good measure.
To smooth your path
along life's way
Would bring me joy
with every day.
But this, alas I cannot do
until I share
your life with you.

Brian A Morris

LIFE'S LOVE

Oh my dear, my love for you, will never cease to be.
Right from the start our love was meant, for God sent you to me.
He knew we'd love one another, and cherish every day.
For love that comes from the very soul, will never go away.

Love will always strengthen the spirit within, so that we learn to share.
And give companionship and love, and show we really care.
For then our hearts will open up, and the love that dwells inside,
Will show the world my gift to you, with a love I need not hide.

And as the years have gently passed, my love for you has grown.
Although you're now with God on high, and sometimes I feel alone.
But deep within this heart of mine, your spirit's still with me.
For our love was a special gift from God, and was always meant to be.

June Margaret Avery

LOVE GLORIFIES

I'm Jack, shepherd lad on the hills,
With skipping lambs, blue-tit trills,
Cupid's dart from Jill's shining hair,
Revealed sweet smiling face so fair.

Her outward charm from love within,
Kindled gladness more than jasmine.
Gone was all loneliness and gloom,
Joy thrilled me, like bee orchid's bloom.

Our eyes met, two hearts fused in love,
To the coppice we freely move;
Sharing our snack on the pure sedge,
Azure skies, dog roses in hedge.

Now Jill is my valentine,
With honeysuckle eglantine.
We have our flock of dappled sheep,
In golden autumn, corn we reap.

Our lives are bound in harmony,
With children's love from self set free.
Happy home with rich blessings share;
Family, neighbours meet us there.

Lovers live with intensity,
Piping times, generosity.
With loyalty we travel on,
Heavenly homeland's goal is won.

James Leonard Clough

LOVE

Sometimes I don't want to live.
You change my mind with the love you give,
You cared for me all the time.
I wanted and needed you to be mine.

You willed me to live, changed my mind,
Introduced me to all things new,
Showed me that I needed to try,
Not just lay down and want to cry.

It's a paper doll situation,
Hearts and bodies tear,
No one sees the hurt,
No one seems to care,

I need you here,
to calm me down
to cheer me up,
and erase my frown,

I often found I couldn't cope,
You showed me a world filled with hope,
Now you're not here, my world has gone,
faded are the lights which brightly shone.

Sometimes I feel I can't cope,
I need someone to care,
Someone who has enough love
Enough for me to share.

Allison Woodhead

THE GREATEST LOVE

A flower is a gift to grace
the earth with perfume and colour,
they're given as a sign of love
from a loved one to another.

A mother will do anything
to rescue her child from danger,
and when he is away from her
worry if he talked to strangers.

A dog will be a faithful friend,
he'll stick close beside his master,
and if he's blind, the dog will sense
if there's impending disaster.

A phone call when you're ill in bed
cheers a sad and lonely heart,
even the smallest note or card
could well play an important part.

Covering a multitude of sins,
it encompasses joy and pain,
like a live electric current
it's never switched off at the mains.

There's no limit to the supply,
the more it's shared, the more it grows,
like ripples on a lake that spreads,
you may not know how far it goes.

Everyone wants to find true love,
so many paths to love are trod,
the greatest love is freely given,
the everlasting love of God.

Mary Care

Towards A Diamond Wedding
September 8 1939 - September 8 1999
(for E F T)

Our love has spanned near sixty years,
In war and peace, in the good times and the bad.
Our vows with sacraments were sealed
And burgeoned through all our hopes and fears
In all our years apart, in the good days and the sad,
In the crises of our lives; in sudden stress concealed.

Our love was blessed with gifts of grace
In direst war, in the longed for end of strife,
In our days together and in our times apart.
In shell-torn hills, I found your face
Serene above the midst of life
And heard your voice within my heart.

We thank our God for all that He has brought
Within our lives, for the laughter and the tears,
For all the days of calm and all our peace at night.
We thank our God for all that he has taught
Through all the movement of the years,
For our enduring love and all its swift delight.

Uvedale Tristram

To Jenny

Some girls, though fair to look upon,
Lack tenderness and grace,
While others, full of warmth and charm,
Are not so fair of face.

But you, dear Jen, the best of all
Fine attributes possess:
Beauty of face and form, combined
With inner loveliness.

John Clark

TOGETHER FOREVER

He's died the man has died
he lay in the bed and died
he wasn't famous he wasn't rich
he just lay there and died alone

She came too late, he lay there still
she'd known him when he'd lived
and breathed danced and sung
to make her laugh and make her cry

But this was all past memories only
memories of joys and sadnesses
together enjoyed together no more
separated but not forgotten memories last

How could she live now he had gone
how could she live when even
breathing was hard to do
when her thoughts were all of him

But she knew that memories and
pictures would sustain her awhile
till her life went to a better place
and they would be forever together.

Barbara Stoneham

I Want . . .

Despite the things you told me and all the things you said,
You're still on my mind, still always in my head.
I wish that I could help you, I want to set you free,
From all that troubles you and holds you back from me.
I want to hold you, I want to feel your touch,
I want you to remember that I love you very much.
I can't help my feelings and they won't just go away,
I want to love you for tomorrow not only for today.
There will be no pressure, I know we can't make plans,
I just want to be there, so let me hold your hand.
I want to share your laughter, I want to share your pain,
I want to stand beside you through the sunshine and the rain.
I want to be there with you whatever life may throw,
My heart cannot desert you, and I just wanted you to know.

Tina Spear

STING

Why was it when we met,
We both remember yet,
The passion stirring deep,
The quantum leap?

Why was it when I sighed,
You hurried to my side,
Across, the pretence gone,
The Rubicon?

Why was it when they said,
That tears would soon be shed,
We hearkened not their call?
Love conquers all!

Why was it when you left,
I felt betrayed, bereft?
Vain Cupid's arrows crossed,
Love's labour's lost.

Why is it when we, now,
Embrace this holy vow,
Pledge spirit, soul and heart,
Till death us part?

Why was it when you died,
I walked alone and cried,
The passion stirring deep,
The quantum leap?

Peter Davies

WHAT IS LOVE? - THIS CURIOUS WORD

To define it, is absurd.
In it's true stature
It can give endless rapture.

It flies like a butterfly,
With many a moan and sigh.
Hidden in shadows and mist,
Like a will-o'-the-wisp.

Unchartered like the depths of the ocean;
As rare as gold is this potion.
Apparently all around,
It is more talked about than found.

Some find it early in life;
Others, after inner strife
Give up, going to their graves
Not having ever discovered
This thing called love.

D A Dart

LOVE'S ACCLAMATION

Love's acclamation to my mind
Began from just a glance
Sun-rays of love that kissed my heart
Love's flame began to dance.
The birth of love a flame for life
Aroused by eyes that gleam,
From heart and mind conveying love,
Love took its hold supreme.

Two hearts, two minds, two lives, one bond
This bond of yours and mine,
Two dancing flames becoming one
More closer than the vine.
This flame of love that fills the heart
A gift to hold and keep,
Until the day love's flame dies out
To rest in happy sleep.

Peter James O'Rourke

MOTHERLY AFFECTION

Love is there in the beginning
Cradled in our mother's arms
With the gentle cooing and reassurance
That we are protected from harm

Mother looks after us as we grow
She guides us along our way
That is why we have
A special Mother's Day

Mother is there when we are grown up
We are never far from her mind
She still remembers us with affection
In our own homes when we left our first one behind

Pauline Edwards

SUNSET

She greeted old friends with a smile, as warm as summer's sun,
And eyes that sparkled into life, not to be outdone.
Her friends were all aware she had so little time to stay,
And sought to bring a touch of cheer to each remaining day.
They felt so helpless, conscious that her strength was on the wane,
But they were welcomed gratefully, as flowers welcome rain.
Propped upright, with smile in place, lips just tinged with red,
She entertained them royally from her throne-like bed.
The mood was always heartening and pity had no place
Around the bed illuminated by her radiant face.
These friendly meetings were for her the highlights of her day,
Until that final morning when she quietly slipped away.
Her face was calm and peaceful while ours, with tears, were wet.
Her smile had gone forever and for us the sun had set.

Frank Jensen

VALENTINE'S WISH

I do not know if you received the message I got of love
Long lost and best forgot

Looking for a new love is so hard to find
I wish I was back with my one and true love
I long left behind

A lass she long passed away and that
I find so hard today to bear
Will I ever find a new love so rare for me to share

I see love all around me, I see love everywhere I go
The love of life, the love of God
But the love of a woman is what I have not!

To be her Valentine, and drink the wine that makes her mine
beauty within that only lovers can begin

But day, by day I sit and pray of love on Valentine's day
A love that seems so very far away and I can't seem to find
The words that could make a woman mine.

Life so empty and bare without a love to share,
No Valentine's card will I become, and one more
year no card to be sprung

So all you people out there that have a lover so true and rare to share
Be sure to show them how much you care

Paul Volante

YOU

Without you, I am nothing
A shadow, just a shell
How much I love you darling,
No words can ever tell.
You are my inspiration
My beacon, shining light.
If only I could hold you,
Each and every night.
This heart of mine beats faster,
Each time I see your face
Your smile is so enchanting,
And you, so full of grace.
You have a sense of humour
Which I admire so much
You may not be aware of it,
My soul, yearns for your touch.
Perhaps we could be happy.
Together you and I
But I could never ask you,
For I am far too shy!

T G Bloodworth

VALENTINE'S

As an old lady of eighty-eight, very nearly eighty-nine,
I remember the thrill of receiving my first valentine,
Trying to guess who the donor might be,
Was it a hoax, or did he truly love me?
The card was so pretty, the words sounded sincere,
I'd have known at once, had the sender been near.
In those days a lifetime's partner was our aim,
Living together was fidelity, not just a game.
Unlike today when couples their lives share,
Flaunting their unmarried state, not having a care.
I had over fifty years of wedded bliss,
Happy memories, over which I reminisce.
I know I'm old-fashioned, but hope lives on,
That love and romance are not something 'bygone',
Maybe a valentine will awaken someone's heart,
To a lifetime of happiness, never to part.

Kathleen Jones

PLEASE

If no one wants what I can give
How can I feel I want to live?
What is the fun of getting up
To make another lonely cup
Of tea?
Somewhere I'm sure there's a man who
Is feeling the same way I do.
Please God give us the luck to meet
And let love make a life complete
For him and me.

Ula Paine

LOVE'S SWEET SONG

Away from city's flashing lights
And fuming traffic roar
Courted Tina, twenty three
And John of twenty four

With no cosy flat or sofa snug
They romanced on rustic bridge
John, he stole a tender hug
Tina sipped Coke from the fridge

On a balmy summer night
Moths did flutter round the light
Their gentle wings were like soft kisses
Pursed by John who rarely misses

Through the long hours, mid perfume of flowers
Couple swayed as John's ardour grew
Though he'd had his ration, he seethed with base passion
And cried 'Let's make one out of two!'

He felt that he must, give way to his lust
Though Tina cried, 'You didn't ought' a'
Her patience and the bridge both broke
And all ended up in the water

Peter N Lawrence

FALLING

'Help I'm falling' were the words cried,
While I stood watching by the roadside,
And like the setting sun she disappeared,
Out of my life, as I was hit by the tears,
I did not reply as I lost my nerve,
For my inner-self was in such a stir.

She had climbed the hill of observance,
But I did not see for I was obsessed,
For it was another that I did see,
And to the one before I now feel sorrow
For us together there is no tomorrow.

For she was falling, for she had just jumped,
But it was a mountain more than a hump,
And so I have caused the death of another,
For I could not see that we could be lovers,
And so I now miss what could have been,
Because the obvious all but I have seen.

Shaun Jeffery

SECRET LOVE

She never knew I loved her
For I loved her from afar.

I didn't ever meet her
My lovely shining star.

I never gave her flowers
Or even touched her hand.

But, to me, she'll always be
The fairest in the land.

She never ever looked at me
Or gave that special glance,

Because she never knew about
Our secret sweet romance.

And now my love is resting
In her island shrine,

But I'll remember all my life
That special love of mine.

Let them take away her title
Or try to change her style,

But one thing they will never change
Is her sweet loving smile.

So now our time is ended,
But from when my story starts,

I know that she will always be
My special Queen of Hearts.

Brian Hope Gent

WITHOUT YOUR LOVE

Falling snow deadens sounds
Frost like dew on full green leaves
pierces the hearts of unborn roses
The playful breeze, an icy blast
The sun, a pale, cold skin on skimming clouds
Birds' songs fade, muted by an indifferent ear
Beauty disregarded by sad non-seeing eyes
Nature desolated
by our parting.

Gloria Geldert

DO YOU EVER TAKE THE BLAME

I was very excited when we became pen-pals
I gave you information with complete honesty.
However since re-reading your work it galls
To find that your obsession with love equals dishonesty.

Roxy, Ruth, Vicky. How many more
Have you declared such undying love?
I am frightened to be added to your score
I know not what He must think in heaven above.

All the poems of love you sent me I have many copies.
Just as I believe did others declaring your wish
Not for a pen-pal or companion to discuss topics
Merely to reel in a woman. Just like a fish.

I cannot believe you seek true love. It seems a must
To accomplish your sole aim to bed each woman.
For your transference from others to me I'm sure is lust.
Like the others I too fell for flattery. Just didn't see you coming.

You are absolutely correct I do not know you.
My compliments on some of your work was genuine acclaim.
Nor do I believe you accepted me as a friend and felt blue
As you poured out your love and tears. Fear caused us to turn against
you.

Time and time again.
Do you ever take the blame?
Have you ever really cared for anyone,
Or are you so conceited you're never wrong.

J Baker

PLEASE BE MY VALENTINE!

As each second
Makes a minute.
As each minute
Makes an hour.
As each hour
Makes a day.
I know beautiful Julie,
I love you more
Than I can say.
Oh! Beautiful Julie.
You are so sweet,
So perfect, so divine!
My dearest, darling,
Beautiful Julie,
Believe me,
I love you so much.
Please be my valentine!

Graham Mitchell

BE MY VALENTINE . . .

When I look into your eyes,
a light inside me shines.
A light so bright
which is hard to hide and hard to find.

For your heart spells out a warm heart,
a heart with lots to give.
With every sound of your beating heart
a love at last to live.

I do not need expensive gifts
or presents of any kind.
For what I have with you's enough
and is very hard to find.

Love itself matches any gift
is something in a heart to send.
For love is for eternity
is something that can never end.

Rebecca Murby

ANNIVERSARY

There was rain in the morning
The sun shone by three.
The family richly gathered
To witness you joined to me.
With hugs and kisses, food and wine
Wedding joy - my valentine.
Five and fifty years have passed
Since cupid fired his dart of love.
Into a marriage truly made -
Blessed by heaven above.

Marnie Connley

ONCE UPON A TIME

I once had someone who I loved
and truly they loved me
and we sat and read together
beneath the tall wild tree
there were flowered woods to
walk in
we laughed sweet smiles and kissed
paused close beside the forest
fence
to seek long looks at bliss
oh boy we loved each other
how swift the hours flew
so bright we clutched at
every day
this was for good we knew
these daytime hours passed away
one kiss beside the shed
just then our mothers' voices
came
calling us to bed

Susan Selby

Valentine

Will you, won't you, become my lover
Say you'll take me into your heart
Surely there can be no reason why
We should be now kept apart.

It was first sight of your beauty
That took possession of me
But the last thing I desire now
Is to be given my liberty.

Captured by bewitching dark eyes
What hope can there be now for me
Or perhaps chance that you might respond
To your unknown lover's plea.

A prisoner of a distant love
How much longer am I to grieve
For only you will have the power
To grant me now my reprieve.

With eagerness I wait for you
Give a token or some sign
To convince me that you have a heart
That's in accord with mine

So please grant me an audience
As soon as it can be done
And meet the heartfelt welcome
Of your lovelorn captive one

Jack W Cash

How Speaks My Love?

Love speaks by giving,
Then by receiving.
Love is a touch and a smile;
Love is a look, a heart to beguile.

Love speaks with laughter,
Moments of rapture!
Love's a caress so divine.
Love is the warmth when those arms entwine.

Love speaks when hearts ache,
Pain longing to take;
There when the world's in despair.
Love always speaks by just being there.

Love speaks by being,
Love speaks by feeling,
Love speaks,
Love is!

Sheila E Harvey

TO THE MEN IN MY LIFE

When I think of all the men in my life,
To one I am a daughter, to one a wife,
Some are just acquaintances, some I do not know,
But all have made a difference and I wish to tell them so.

Thank you for your strong, warm arms and shoulders where I cried,
Thank you for the wars you fought, where some of you died,
You built the roads and baked my bread,
You gave me love, and shared my bed.

You cared for me when I was ill,
Worked hard to pay every bill,
Delivered milk and washed my floors,
Made me feel special by opening doors.

Some men are fun and make me laugh,
One has been my 'better-half',
You drilled my teeth or mended my car,
Do you know how wonderful you are?

My father and my teachers taught me what is right,
Policemen and firemen working through each night,
Soldiers and others so brave and so strong,
Working to protect me, all night long.

Thank you for your company and for being my friend,
My love for you will surely never end,
You asked me out on that first date,
And many years later I am still your mate.

Thank you for listening and trying and caring,
For helping and loving, for buying and sharing,
To all the men in my life, what ever you do,
I want you to know that - *I love you!*

C M Kemp

VALENTINE'S DAY

Today he smiled
With warmth and care,
Charming me,
Beguiling.

Response I gave
Was quite aloof.
As if he was not there,
Passed him by
Innocent - with flare.

We met again
Another day
Surprising each other, it's true,
Fate seemed to map our paths,
Mingling and entwining.

This day I woke
Tradition says,
First man you see
Will marry.

Imagine my delight,
Viewing from my window
The man who was not there
Stood smiling,
I just could not ignore him.

Lorna Tippett

THE SEASON OF LOVE

Spring is drawing near - it's the season of love.
Love is God's most precious gift, sent from above.
Valentine's day is very special too
Romance stirs in your heart -
Love is in the air - but that is nothing new.

Lovers strolling hand in hand in the park
Waiting for the day to end - so they can make
                              love in the dark
It's that wonderful time of year.
When we send Valentine cards too.
Full of words showing our love
For each other - so easy to do.

'To my Valentine' the cover of the card will say.
Although in days gone by 'a secret admirer'
                              his respects would pay
Welcome spring - so glad you are near
And the season of love is once again here.

Marjorie Ridley

GIRLFRIEND

Girlfriend
awaken me
from this sleepy summer's dream
and speak of forgotten England.
Then lay the rose upon white cotton
and quench the thirst
of awkward innocence.

Michael Wilson

REFLECTION

I looked out from my window
and saw you were not there
not the smell of your nearness
nor the fold of your hair
not the light in your eyes
or dances to hypnotise
no fingers to curl
a window which is bare

I looked out from my window
to the distant trees
silhouetted against the sky
with an ever moving breeze
I watched the sun turn from
an early morning ball
the glow held in my heart
but you're not there at all

I looked out from my window
from my sheltered heart within
and wondered 'why' I ever let you in
somewhere on our beach
your voice will wait for me
when I look up at my window
your face is all I see . . .

Jenny Bickers

ANGEL OF MINE

Always and forever, he could be mine,
Everyday, until the end of time.

People say 'He's not for you,'
but what do they know? they don't have
a clue.

He is perfect in every way,
I think I'll set the wedding for the
end of May . . .

I guess I can wait until he's single,
and then once again my heart will tingle.

Kellymarie Richmond (14)

I HEARD HIS VOICE

I heard his voice say tenderly
'Come to me and rest.'
And so in confidence I lay
my head upon his breast.

I looked up to my love and found
in him my star, my light.
And by that star, in life I'll walk
straight through the darkest night.

Fay Smith

THAT MOMENT

We met by chance that sunny day
And chatted as we went our way
And from that moment everything
Was like a lovely breath of spring,
For he was handsome, tall and fair
Whose company was fun to share,
And as we talked his lovely smile
Made every moment so worthwhile,
I noticed then my beating heart
Quite suddenly was taking part
In something very strange to me
It caught my breath! What could it be?
And when he slipped his hand in mine
Well, everything was so divine,
We wandered on at casual pace
Oblivious of time and place,
And then he gently took my arm
Affectionately and with such charm
Then, closer still, that lingering kiss
Changed my whole life, but more than this
His twinkling eyes so clear and blue
Told me a dream had just come true
More precious than all else above -
That moment, when, we fell in love.

Evelyn Jones

MY KIND OF MAN

There are men who smoke and also 'booze'
They're not the type that I would choose.
Men with money, great physique
Are not the kind that I would seek.
Others with great strength of mind
Again, my choice is not this kind
My gentle, ordinary you,
The only one for me, would do!

Margaret Rankin

FATE

Deep within the forest of life
I was frightened and feeling alone.
I knew not where I was going.
I felt the seeds of fate had been sown.

You extended a line to me
And broke up my old daily routine.
You remain so dependable,
Perhaps destiny is not so mean.

Steal away my heart and my dreams,
Show me that nothing is ever planned,
Tell me that I can live it all -
Just grasp each single moment in hand.

Time dictates that we all must change
For yesterday is never today.
I must appreciate you now
In case by some chance you slip away.

Barbara Pearce

...JUST LIKE A BREATH

The breath
In your words
Hold me,
Bringing a truer
Meaning to the word
Love.

Like a breath
Of fresh air
I'll always find
You there
Not hiding in the shadows
But smiling into the
Windows of my soul.

Susi Briggs

ODE TO A LOST LOVE

You have gone
I am left,
All dreams shattered
Heart bereft.
Once a pair
Now alone,
Words of anger,
Now you're gone.
All this sadness
Tears and pain,
Things will never
Be the same,
How I miss you
Can you know,
Please come back
I love you so.

L McLeish

UNTITLED

'I love you' he said to me, as he leaned across to clasp my hand
A conversation tonight, I really hadn't planned.

Then suddenly the atmosphere stilled and I was in the bar alone
The volume of rowdy drunkens silenced and became a peaceful moan.

And then it happened, the heavens opened and right before my eyes
A thousand sweet singing angels floated slowly from the skies

Each playing on small golden harps and fluttering their wings
Making pretty motions in the air and scattering pink and golden things

Which fell and settled in my hair and made me twinkle too
And enabled me to then leave the floor and fly like angels do

And up and up, and up we went, up so very high
And I cushioned myself on a cloud with silver lining in the sky

In fact I should have sussed it then, you'd have thought at that
point I'd twig
For it wasn't the unicorn that followed after that, it was in fact
the flying pig

That sent me hurtling back down again falling undaintily to the ground
To meet the familiar gathering of publicans and the drunken
rowdy sound.

Of a bell being rung quite loudly and 'last orders' being
bellowed out loud
And no longer had I the comfort of my silver lining cloud

And I came to the realisation that even after those 3 special words
The whole experience was mere fiction and had never even occurred

'Well . . .' he said with slight hesitation as he looked me in the eye
As I raised my head and our eyes met, I knew I couldn't lie

And as if having succumbed to one of life's long joke
'Next time,' I whispered in his ear, I think I'll leave off that double
Vodka and Coke.

Vicky Dillingham

FROM DARK TO LIGHT

Never having known love
I knew not if I loved you
As a child I spoke

Never touching love
How can I experience affection
As a child I spoke

A simple smile, fond words
Locked from me
As a child I spoke

Searching home's hidden corners
Finding only cobwebs of loneliness
As a child I spoke

Solitary black shadow
Following tiny footsteps of sadness
As a child I spoke

You are my first trust
Guide this husk from dark to light
As a childlike adult I spoke

You saw what I did not
Seeds of love within a hidden heart
Sleeping until woken by your caress
As a man I spoke

Embrace me tightly with your love
Amorous lips meeting, exploding
Such beauteous sensations
Flooding my being

Gaze upon my face
Behold a vision of tenderness
Expressing my love for you
Now, as your husband I speak.

D A Watson

EMOTIONALLY CHARGED

I danced naked, on my birthday.
Nobody else was there but him.

We had just woken up.
I put some music on . . .

I felt like taking off my night clothes,
I felt like dancing . . . dancing . . .

Dancing naked, on my birthday.
Around the bed.

Under his very eyes.
He said, he didn't mind.

I was celebrating
The love I had in my heart.

Dancing around the bed, I was celebrating
The love I had in my heart.

I danced naked, on my birthday.
Nobody else was there but him.

'You make me feel like a man' he told me.
I was celebrating . . . our love . . .

Claire-Lyse Sylvester

ONE FINE DAY

You wake
> To the crunch of wheels on gravel
>> The slam of a car door

And you imagine him
> With suitcase and guitar
>> The only dowry he ever said he'd bring

> Then grinding silence . . .

But one fine day, you think -
> Switch on the radio
>> And find she's there too

Madam Butterfly
> Singing Puccini
>> Long into the desperate night.

Margaret Ericsen

THE HONOUR OF LOVE

Love is a wonderful romantic thing,
Great expectations to your heart it brings,
Those longings that it will last,
As the poundings of your heart runs fast.

Love can bring heartache and tears too,
Like if your loved one has to leave you,
Like my love, who once sailed the seas everywhere,
But our thoughts for each other were always there.

Love then means everything,
Even across the world, there is thought and care,
Through those passages of life,
Time has made *love* stronger you see.

Once told I was surrounded by water,
How true that came to be . . .
May others find that *love* that has been given to me,
As older you get . . . may you never regret.

We took an oath together . . .
Both my sailor valentine and I,
Now he is at home, and tells me everyday,
'I love you and our little anchorage home,
We live only half a mile from the coast,
Knowing while we have each other, now is the greatest and the most.

Anita M Slattery

WHAT IS LOVE

Love is true,
Love is sweet,
Love is deep,
Love is caring,
Love conquers,
Love survives,
Love is abiding,
Love is formidable,
Love rides the storms of adversity,
Love climbs the troughs of despair,
Love is the greatest gift we possess
And without it, we are nothing.

Dorothy Schofield

ROMANCE TO THE DANCE

Shrugging off the coldness of Winter's dress,
Those dark longed filled evenings now grown less.
Migrations wings of birds' return,
Thawing of nature, new beginnings burn.

The first lambs soon to patchwork the hills,
A beam of sunlight still an early spring chill.
Wisp of clouds on satin blue sky,
Prism of colour, fragrances high.

Laughter in the wind chance of rain it might bring,
Beauty of hope, romance sings.
Peace and tranquillity serenades the calm,
As heart young and old, fall in love with its charm.

Dreamy evenings of candlelight, roses and wine,
Starry eyed lovers, hearts entwined.
Fires of passion as thoughts read as one,
A moment to last, togetherness has come.

Whispers of happiness, two lovers adore,
First moonlit walk on glittering shores.
Treasured felt love fragile as Ming,
The wonder of magic in the returning of spring.

Audra Ann Murphy

VALENTINE'S DAY

See the cards come through the door
is there one or many more.
You get roused when you read the words
your heart flutters like wings of a bird.
Cards with red hearts and flowers
Cupid's little bows and arrows.
Loving feelings in every one
or just sent for teasing fun.
An admirer from the past
or a love you hope will last.
Who wrote this scribbled name?
Did you send one just the same?
A loving heart knows no age
whether young or older stage.
There's a flutter deep inside
these feelings you cannot hide.
All sent with love, good wishes
and in the corner - lots of kisses.

S Waller

I NEED YOU

I need you in the morning
Beside me when I awake
The warmth of your body
So my love you can take.
I want to know you care for me
And feel the way I do
Touching each other gently
For happiness to shine through
I need you in the daytime
To think of me at work
Earning money for us both
So we can buy our perks.
Time passes slowly knowing you aren't here
But you're always on my mind
I can't help myself and wipe away a tear
I need you in the evening
To hold you in my arms
Caressing you affectionately
Admiring all your charms
Do you think of me often while I'm away?
Whisper the words I long for?
I love you today
I need you at night time
When it is time for bed
Next to me under the sheets
And rest my weary head
Close your eyes and dream of me
And the love we have to share
Wake me up at daybreak
And show me again how much you care.

Jan Nice

LOVERS

Oh! So lucky,
With all the universe around
Moon and stars we like magnets
Drawn together found a love
With no bars, sweet scented to last forever.

Oh! So lucky,
In young love when fair of face
Met eyes of brown
In culture and the same race
And knew we were meant for each other.

Oh! So lucky,
Committed to that band of gold
Swore to honour, love, cherish
And obey. There was never any doubt
Feelings just the same - loving one another.

Oh! So lucky,
To understand, and be understood
To find a deeper love can grow
If seeds you sow are trust and honesty.
Peace of mind as you only could.

Oh! So lucky,
Four children we have, and they the nest
Have flown, and now have children of their own.
We worked hard to share our dream
Find happiness is to smile, be gentle and kind
And memories are the hearts of gold.

Gwen Haines

REFLECTIONS

I missed you in Donegal -
Though I don't love you now,
Somehow
I missed you in Donegal.

I missed having you by my side
In the turf fire's soft glow,
Long ago,
I missed you in Donegal.

I missed the strong clasp of your hand,
When I walked in the glen
'Twas then
I missed you in Donegal.

I missed you where moon shadows fall
And in pale light at dawn,
Gone, gone,
I missed you in Donegal.

Patricia Neill

ONE

You
you mean
so much
so much to me
to me
you
only you
bring happiness
tenderness
warmth
caring
I
want to be
with you
with only you
day and night
your happiness
my happiness
our happiness
body and soul
you to me
me to you
One.

Patrick Miller

FATED LOVE

When we met it was a twist of fate,
You came into my life too late.
You already belonged to another,
From this fate I had to recover.

You were there in my troubles,
Always at my side.
And though the rose of summer,
Had wilted and gone.
My feelings for you just went on and on.

You were companion and friend,
My heart started to mend.
You were my life's guide,
Remaining steadfast by my side.

In your window I'd see a light,
As you worked, far into the night.
Your own inner light shone on so bright,
Yet I worried, something did not seem right.

The day finally came when your candle burnt out.
Helping others you'd told me, is what life's about.
You helped who you could, and you'd given your all.
Though you've gone on ahead, memories I recall.

I'll never forget you, you were my best friend,
And though I can't see you, I know you're around.
I feel your presence with me,
And my heart with joy does abound.

I know you're still with me.
Your body has gone, but your spirit is free.
I hear your voice, and this gives me,
Cause to rejoice.
For you're now free from pain,
And I know one day, I'll see you again.

Hilary Ann Torrens

MY LOVE

When we were younger,
Love was so exciting,
Ecstasy and sometimes despair.
New things we were discovering,
So many things we could compare.

When we were married,
Love was more demanding.
With children there was need to share
The trials of daily living
Meant there was less time to spare.

Now we are older
Why, my love is deepening.
Of thoughtful ways I am aware
Of little faults more forgiving.
Now I need to show I care.

Patricia Eales

REFLECTIONS OF YOU

I am looking back now,
with memories of gold.
'Honest' golden times together,
we both, did richly hold.

Two beautiful children,
I treasure, to give my love too
for in their beautiful faces
I see reflections of you.

Maybe, it was an act of fate,
maybe, a weakness of soul
maybe, my unforgiveness,
that lead us to this role.

But I do wish you well,
I hope you wish me well too.
Maybe, someday we find happiness,
like the way we used to do.

Let us look forward, not back at the past
for this pain in my heart must surely not last
someday I may find love again, and love you find too
build a family with happiness like our parents did do.

Ken Draffin

LOVE'S REASONS

I went into her bedroom,
and got it off her chest.

Read a book on depression
and now I am depressed.

There's a psychological reason
for being physically ill.

All the nonsense in the world
for running and standing still.

Cupboards, chairs, and wardrobes
viewed in hesitation,

Go off at a tangent
to make a reservation.

So I close your door, behind me:
forget a memory span.

Meditate less often now,
than when I was a man.

David Hazlett

FLASHBACK

Amidst the tumble of imposing order
On chaos
I fell to the floor
On my face
And stole one sparkling silent moment
When disharmony faded out.
The room seemed brighter
That one sweet instant
That I first saw you.
Invisible hands
Bore me to my feet.
It all seemed weightless
On that perfectly bad day
That you came along and ruined.

Rumana Kabir (17)

TO MY VALENTINE

'Oh, my dear valentine
Your eyes seem so far away, just look into mine
Why do you look so sad, when our eyes meet
When I draw closer to you, show no defeat

When I draw near, I brush your brow
Now, my love, you are smiling, now
With the love I bring
Come, now and dance and sing
Under the stars, that shine so bright
Oh, my valentine, through this romantic night

With your brows now high
No matter how you have been, don't sigh

I am still standing near, with love I bring
So near, but yet so far, but, to me you are everything
Even times when you wander oh, love of mine
You are my one, my seen secret valentine.

Kathleen Spilsbury

THE LOVE OF MY LIFE

You are my sun, moon and the stars,
as night follows day
you have never been away
my fears subside
when you are near
it encompasses my soul
and makes me whole.

We travel together a sensuous road
where skies are ever blue
and bird song everywhere
an orchestra of shining voices
laying a carpet of trust
to secret places
where our hearts can roam.

Fulfilling vows, seeking happy
places to lay our heads,
orange blossom to tie the knot
a garland of sentimentality
and happy voices
for which the marriage
of true minds, rejoices.

Joan Hands

BE MY LOVE

This must be love, this wonderful emotion,
That stirs my soul, puts stars into my eyes,
And leaves me restless, yearning for the loved one,
Yet all I do is fill the air with sighs!

I cannot sleep or concentrate on duty,
My heart is throbbing madly all the day,
I long to know the answer from my loved one,
If only I could find the perfect way.

How do I know that this is really true love,
Long-lasting, for a lifetime, and forever?
Because I cannot live if we are parted,
Please say that we will always be together!

If you consent to share the future with me,
Then I will care for you for ever more,
So in this poem I give my dedication -
'Tis you I love, and cherish, and adore.

Joan Letts

BUT WHAT IF?

I think he likes me,
But maybe he doesn't,
Guess what, he said hello!
Should I ask him or wait to be asked?
I don't know what to do!
Maybe my friend could ask him,
But then he might laugh and tell his mates that I like him!
But I do,
Oh I do,
Yes I definitely do,
So tell him,
But what if he hates me?

(Hello? . . . Are you still there? . . . Hello? . . .)

Just forget it!

Sophie Ball

A ROSE FOR MY TRUE LOVE

The symbol of my love for you
Must be a scarlet rose.
Just like our love it never dies
For on and on it grows.
With the softness of each petal
I compare your tender touch,
Such pure and natural beauty
Like the love I feel so much.
The stimulating fragrance
Of nature's sweet perfume,
To fill my senses just as if
You walked into the room.
Deep red to show the passion
We both feel for each other.
Each pretty bloom unique, like you,
There could not be another.
To give and to receive a rose
Will show our ever love,
Both sent with every blessing
From heaven up above.

Helen Hill

REALIZATION

Am I to cast aside those moments
Breathing in the life of my sleeping dreams
Only to feel the emptiness of your goodbye -
Searching for your face amidst the scattered
Crowd I realize how I need to feel the
Familiarity of you being with me -
Sadly it's what I want yet I still create
Illusions for myself as I disperse the
Reality of this union,
Waiting for the shadow of my heart
To return to its ghost-life existence.

Donna Burns

NATURE AND LOVE

Without love it's night-time, dark and forlorn,
Empty of warmth that is absent till dawn
The coldness surrounds you, chills to the bone
The iciness bites you, when you are alone.

Sunrise is an awakening it opens your eyes
Love begins to seep through you as the sun does the sky
It surrounds you completely, every part of your world
Like the sun to the earth, as the morning's unfurled.

Noon is the point when the sun is most strong
Your love is now perfect, you can do no wrong
The passion's abundant, there's love all around
Love beats down on you like the sun on the ground.

Sun cycle comparisons begin to end here
Love continues to flourish as sunset draws near
It survives all adversities, it continues right through
Night can never destroy it if your love is true.

Rebecca Stanley

Ruby Wedding

Remember when we were young dear, our love about to start.
With all our lives before us, sure of step and light of heart.
To share our lives together, we vowed in church that day.
So much to learn about each other, the first step on the way.

But now we're so much older. Oh how the time has flown.
Each care we've shared together, and every joy we've known,
Has left its mark upon us, silver hair and furrowed brow.
There is one consolation, I love you much more now.

The years have brought us closer, where some have grown apart.
They have bound us close together. One single beating heart.
That shows us how our feelings are so much stronger now.
How we care for each other, every day, some way, some how.

And as my footsteps falter, one thing alone is sure.
One constant bright conclusion, that I just love you more.
So keep this thought before you. It hasn't been in vain.
If I only had the chance, then I would do it all again.

Norman Brookes

BACKPACKER KISSES

It's more that just a kiss.
At the same point
On different journeys,
Lonely hands reaching out
Across thousands of miles,
Feeling for familiarity in
Intimacy, but burying love
That makes parting painful.

Just someone to hold on to
Hold you on a tropical night,
Soft sand sticking to moist
Bodies briefly illuminated
By a distant beacon;
Transient touching and then
Leaving in different directions,
And like our shadows in the sand
Tomorrow we will be gone,
Moving on.

David Atkinson

THE LOVE WE KNEW

The far moon haunts me, but makes lovers wise
As my memories still dwell, still thinking of your dark eyes
In my dreams, I still see your form standing there so strong
And, how our hearts beat fast, when those nights were young

Strangeness came over us, when we shared our first kiss
Magic was in the air, as the joy we felt, and such bliss
As, we stood alone together, under the pale moonlight
I still imagine your face shadow over me, through that starry height

Slowly, silently, the moon moved around the trees
The silvery moon shone with the light breeze
So romantic was that night, precious and sweet
Just the two of us, no one was in sight, so quiet was the street

The night was mysteriously dimming, as you held me close,
No sound, but the phrasing of the nightingales rich notes
Through that mid summer's night, my dreams still remember
The flames were on fire, through that love for each other

Remembering, the warm days, as we strolled by the river side
My shining eyes looked up to you, those things I just couldn't hide
The flames were so bright, as you whispered in my ear
Those three wonderful little words, that I loved to hear

When your lips met mine, the innocent love was free from guilt
When your fingers ran through my hair, golden moments were built.
But gone is that rare love, as it went passing by
Like a bird in the open air, flying through a motionless sky

Out of my arms, into my dreams, whenever dark shadows fall
But still, the far moon makes lovers wiser, when nature calls
And another love came into my heart, like the risen sun
When Jesus Christ came into my life, and will be there till day is done.

Jean P McGovern

WHEN YOU'RE IN LOVE

When you're in love
Cupid shoots his arrows from above
Arrows flying everywhere
When you're in love you just don't care
When you go to a disco in hope of romance
A gorgeous boy asks you to dance
You feel quite strange, your heart starts to race
As you dance with your dream date
Then you arrange to meet him again
You arrange a time, where and when
You get there and your dream comes true
Your date's got a red rose waiting for you
When you break up you start to cry
But no-one understands the reason why
And next week you forget that romance
When another dream date asks you to dance!

Cheri Hopkins (15)

ANGEL OBSESSION

With the smile of an angel and the eyes of a saint,
Her face would glow from morning till night,
I couldn't help but fall for her - throughout my teenage flight.

Her hands were woven from satin, a touch that felt like silk,
They worked on me from near and far - I watched her every movement,
I fell in love my first teenage year.

The mornings I would wake up cold, I needed her warm smile,
Her beauty touched my heart so deep - although I never told,
My time with her I'll always keep.

I took her subject twice a day, mesmerised in class I'd sit,
I never learnt what others would be taught, but learned of love -
different kind
No-one must know, I can't be caught.

I slowly grew obsessed with her, and let it rule my mind,
A mad young girl in love, I became - I bottled it inside,
Who could I tell of my great shame.

I couldn't see the harm in love, abandoned though it seemed.
It threw itself upon me - yet so kind
Others would see wrongly, I knew inside my mind.

Weakened, I faced upon it, indirectly was my aim,
I told her of my secret plight - and how I was so proud,
For my love, beliefs and feelings I would fight.

She touched my arm without a thought, and told me it was life,
'A part of growing up,' she said - 'My phase would pass eventually'
She never knew my phase took her, with me, to bed.

I left her in my search for life, though I crushed upon her beauty,
I found her eyes in everyone I came to know - and trusted all,
Eventually my fantasy would go and leave a clearer mind.

I'm 'better' now, more comforted, I'm 'straight' in where I'm going,
I've settled down in love and life - I took the path that pleased me.
And now live happily with my wife!

Vivienne Bern

Searching For Love

I wake up lonely, cold and afraid,
Gone is the love that you once gave.
I reach out for you, but you're not there,
There's nobody to hold me, nobody to care.

Through the darkness I begin to cry,
Remembering the night when you kissed me goodbye.
You stole my heart, then broke it in two,
You left me alone to live without you.

The emptiness I feel is tearing me apart,
I know, to you, I have lost my heart.
You taught me the greatest dreams can die,
And showed me it felt to cry.

I never knew love could cause so much pain,
I never knew tears could fall like rain.
But I'll keep on searching for someone to hold,
Someone to love me and keep out the cold.
For I know somewhere he waits for me,
Somebody who's hurting just like me.

Claire Marie Harris

THE FIRST THING

The first thing is
That your thoughts
Take over your sense
Even though you live
In double or triple
The best is when
Your thoughts think
And it does not matter
If they are weak or robust

When thoughts think not
In the tedium you can hear
Your own questions or other's
By which the calm can be lost

And you can think
Why I was not born
Long before or later
Did my mother like me
Much more than my father?
Why have you got
Or have you not got
A brother or sister
Maybe everything
Life
Family
Love
Are ordered things
And easily comes
An absence of calm

Fahrija Hodzic

MEMORIES

Remember once when you and I were young;
When love was life, and life stretched endlessly?
How little, then, we knew of time's cruel ways -
How, coming in between, she would sever you from me.
And yet, though you are gone, through all my tears
The memory of your smile still haunts my days;
And when life drives turmoil's arrows to my heart
I'll find peace in your soft, remembered gaze.

Beryl Laithwaite

LOVE AND THE UNSUNG HERO: A TRIBUTE TO GEORGE

He rises at the dawn,
pulls open the curtain,
now knowing for certain
his work starts again this very morn.

His wife, laid low in her middle age
now depends on his loving care.
Their home, now becoming a living cage,
this illness has robbed her of her wifely share,
of what over fifty years they did together.

He must get her up, bathe and feed her,
dress her, make her look as smart as he can,
this caring devoted loving man.
He cooks, cleans and gardens too,
always with a loving smile for her,
his wife and partner too.
If what I see when they are together,
is not *love* then *I* must be blind.

Kathleen Collins

MY VALENTINE

As we approach St Valentine's Day once more,
The stirrings in my heart are as before.
Never far away am I, from your side.
You are my life, my mentor, and my guide.
Next year will surely shine - as ruby marks the date;
And looking back along those years,
You've been the perfect mate.
A family we've raised, and now with
Grandsons, four,
Our love has spread its wings,
As it encircles all.
I don't need to ask - 'Will you be mine?'
Indeed I know; My Valentine.

Anne Baker

MEMORIES

When the periodic table would turn,
you'd hold me close, rubbing my back
with your healing hands and soothing words.

When you'd whisper those comforting words
'I love you', suddenly the metamorphosis
from pain to love

When you'd tickle me all over and I'd try
hard to resist, but never could . . .
I never wanted too.

When you'd nibble and whisper erotically in my ear,
taking me into another world,
another dimension of feelings.

When we'd play those silly word games,
you'd always come out on top,
but I let you.

Somewhere along the line our words
became entangled in a sea of mesh.
They embedded in the sand banks,
losing all weight and volume.

You grew away from me, my growth was stunted.
I've grown now, not fully,
I still have a few stretch marks to bare.

K McLaine

LOVE HURTS

Love is a wonder to me
It makes us fight and argue you see
Love is very clear to me, we had built
Our future on it don't you see.

Our fights bring tears and sadness deep
In my heart
My heart is heavy with hidden love locked
Now deep within.
How I wish the arguing would end
So I could enter in and find the key
Unlock my love for all to see and then
Throw away my key for all eternity.

It hurts so much when love is harsh, hurtful
And angry it makes me despise myself,
Can you not see what you're doing to me?

The memories I hold dear to me are still
Bright and sparkling,
I want them to be reality once more and close
The door on uncertantity for you and me.

Love is a happiness in my soul
I won't give up it is my goal.

S A Ibrahim

A NEVER-ENDING OCEAN WITH WAVES

Love is a never ending ocean,
With waves that ripple on a moon-lit shore
That laps upon the rocks -
Silently, gently, yet with a dominant feeling.
It can be rough like a stormy sea
That tosses and rushes with great strength.
It can also be calm and collective
With not a movement yet so full of life.
Love, like an ocean
Holds many, many adventures unknown to man
Unless they are discovered
By a courageous mind and body.
Love is like an ocean.
It is all over the world -
And will never become a thing of the past.

Gary Cahoon

SWEET SURPRISE

When beauty doth our hearts awake
And time like mist seems light with ray,
There are no words to speak our sake
Nor thoughts or sound to mar our day;
But hearing tune from hidden dell
Our spirits start to rise and fall
As ships that ride an ocean swell,
That vast expanse without a wall.

Such loving face and smiling eyes,
Honeyed hair and shape serene
My heart is full of sweet surprise
Imbibing beauty; nay, a queen,
Composing muse within my soul
The tunes for many years ahead
When life may sound a duller toll
Than pealed by bells when we were wed.

John Carr

FIRST LOVE, LAST LOVE

Sweet laughter lines, which at the corners grow;
Now silver gleams where once ripe corn did show;
Those warming hands which then my breast would hold;
And gathering arms my body would enfold;
That glinting eye now shines with kindly love;
Those rousing tones now soothe, like murmuring dove.
The gentle comfort of our friendship deep
Does tenderly our precious loving keep.

Annette van Oppen

THE CRYSTAL BALL

A fortune teller told me you loved me
You love me in secret from afar
I long to hear you declare your love
Held close beneath a galaxy of stars

I want to hold out my hand and touch you
Do you know how much I care?
I want to be with you forever
You laughter and tears I want to share

The fortune teller said I act distant
That's why you stay away
I'm frightened to look into your eyes
Fear of rejection stands in my way

I pray you'll become telepathic
Hear these words I cannot express
I feel so alone when I'm not near you
Convert these tears of sorrow . . . to happiness.

Rebecca Lawrence

HEAVENLY SCENT

Hyacinths both pink and blue
Florets heavy with morning dew
Compose a symphony of yesteryear
When you were there.

Regrets unwind remember with
Joy the sweet perfume of God's
Garden treasure and to live
Complete in Jesus now
Is 'love' beyond measure.

M W Clarke

THE IMAGE

I have seen her
She is of a desire
I thought long dead.
Of a thousand ghosts
She stands in vivid pulse
To my seeking eyes.
Pearl teeth and round -
Uncrinkled azure stare.

She looks a gentle queen
Tall, and with an untaught grace,
She passes, and leaves
The thrill of encounter,
And impression on the mind
That kindles soft desire.

I have seen her crimson blush,
Have heard her laughter, soft
That warms my feelings
Into a glow of kinship.
She is of my need: Alas
She is another's love
And of another world.

Henry J Green

THE VALENTINE CARD

Love came along in the thirties,
For my boyfriend Jim and me,
We got on well together,
Then one day he sent to me . . .

A card with coloured ribbon bows,
And each ribbon had a sign,
To send the colour back to him,
The one which said 'You'll be mine.'

The one I sent right back to him,
Was the one of palest blue,
That colour bow was meant to prove,
That to him I would be true.

The next week we met each other,
And went to the jewellers shop,
Came out with an engagement ring,
We really felt over the top.

That day was the fourteenth of Feb.,
'Twas also St Valentine's day,
And - for fifty eight years since then,
Together we've gone the same way.

Isobel Crumley

SPRING FEVER

Why does my heart beat?
Why do I
Stop and gaze and look and sigh?
In winter I was quite content
Apart from Yuletide merriment
To live routinely and not yearn
That romance once again return.

That bird out there has found its mate
I wonder what will be my fate?
Will someone find beyond resisting
This erstwhile lass who's just exciting?

Oh shall I bid my heart be quiet
Or will love's favours soon supply it?
And send to me that special one
Who'll fill my life with love anon.

J Facchini

SITTING HERE

Sitting here,
All I can think of is you,
Sitting here,
All I can see is you,
Sitting here,
All I can hear is you,
Sitting here,
All I need is you.

Qurathulane Beg

OLD LOVE

Can I come to you, so worn
Like a weary worker in a field?
Shall you lift a hand of scorn,
Your lips, no longer loving, sealed?
Shall your eyes look past my brow
Where silver shows its dubious worth?
You loved me once; what of now
When present spring renews the Earth?
Flowers bud like yesterdays'
Remembered blossom times when we
Treated love like youthful craze
Yet swore perpetual loyalty.
Shall you trace my lined old cheek
With gentleness and comprehend
And reprove not when you speak,
As though our romancing must end?
Suddenly I know you more,
Your character of splendid oak,
Shall our love be like before
When words of mutual love we spoke?
Lord, prove me not wrong, but I
This simple man adore,
He'll not pursue the reason why
I am glamourous maid no more.
Can a heart that beats so fast
As mine at even the thought of him
Even more enrich what's past
And constant love refuse to dim?

Ruth Daviat

LOVE IS . . . ?

What is love?
Is it all roses and violets.
Or is it deeper?

Does it come from fathoms below,
Where your heart, soul and mind
Become one?

Does it lightly brush your life?
Or does it drag you to its feet,
Leaving you begging for mercy?

Does it appear in your thoughts occasionally?
Or does it occupy your mind,
Like poisonous ivy?

Is it a wonderful feeling,
Where you float among the stars,
And swing from silver moon-shafts?

Does it contaminate your life,
With difference and strangeness?
Does it stir your imagination?

The only certain thing,
Is that you create it.

Emily Wilson

FOR YOU

When your skin touches mine,
My skin aches -
For you.

When your eyes meet mine,
My heart skips a beat -
For you.

When you are absent from my gaze,
My mind wanders; filled with thought -
For you.

When you are with me
I feel complete and beautiful,
But only for you.

Emma Cottell

VALENTINE

My darling,
(So the writer goes.
But who it's from
No one knows)
I love you with all my heart -
But how could such a romance start?
I long to be held in your arms
And told I have many charms.
I hope you feel this way too,
And love me as I love you.
So ends this message
Of hopeful bliss -
Finishing with a loving kiss . . .

Mary Pauline Winter

THE AGES OF LOVE

When love is new it sparkles like the sunshine after rain,
It fills your head with bubbles like a glass of pink champagne,
You welcome every morning, whether skies are grey or blue,
And you just can't wait to tell the world that somebody loves you.

When love is getting older, it takes on a brand new hue,
You promise love undying and believe it to be true,
You may not always find each other's feeling match your own,
But somewhere deep inside, you feel together and at home.

Your future lies before you and you both have hopes and dreams
But problems, disappointments just don't enter in your schemes.
To face them all together is the underlying key,
For, clearly when all's said and done, then 'What will be will be.'

To reach old age as man and wife means lots of give and take,
You have to compromise, try hard, both for each others sake,
Your love will endure anything if it is wise and true,
So be content, laugh, cry and love - together till life's through.

Carol Drewry

LOVE FOREVER

Touch hands, let our minds move together.
Our thoughts drift in peace
Think not of the sorrow,
Of parting, think of the joy of return.
So summer days slip past,
Unknown to lovers' minds
And unaware they drift towards
The splitting of two lives.
Who will be changed when we meet again?
'Not I,' they vow together,
Will love grow weak and fade?
No we shall love forever.

Joan Patrickson

FRIENDS

Why do we say 'just' friends?
How can we belittle it so
When it's such a wonderful feeling
To have a real, true friend?

True friendship is beautiful, heaven-sent,
And those of us who've found it
Should celebrate its bounteous gift,
Of deep and pure platonic love.

Bridget Holding

I LOST MY LOVE

I lost my love on a misty-heavy night.
We stood in the halo of a streetlamp wreathed in flowers
Angry and fencing with words like sabres
Anxious to hurt and not be hurt,
To prick the bubble of an alien aura
And watch the elemental life-force drain
From its cocoon whilst preserving intact
The angst-laden temper - over what I cannot remember
And so in a moment, I pricked my own bubble
And drowned my heart in sorrow
To live with regret:
'You were happy; you had that; what if you had never met?'
They mean well, I know, but he left
As I lost my love on that starless night.

Carmela Carr

SILHOUETTES

How many pebbles my love;
How many and how few?
How many stars above;
How many there are new?

Has not heaven possessed
Lovers that touch the waves,
Could hubble find a chest
Of lovers' games and plays.

Older we may be, who
Yet at once were young,
Gave life that cradled two,
When mirrored likeness sprung.

I who passion desire you
In the shadow of Portsea,
Where moonlight silvers you -
Silhouettes touch the sea.

Endless love may falter -
Words, token and alter,
My love is all that I knew;
Tears are many and few.

Robin Pearcey

LOVE TO INFINITY

Love is a dictionary of words
Which Cupid's arrow gives new meaning.
A book of infinite chapters
Inspired by the tragic love of Romeo and Juliet

An endless game of chance
Where two players follow the rules of Venus
Each hoping to win the affections of the other
For a moment of love that will last a lifetime

A letter written with the pen of Aphrodite
Reflecting a heart's ocean of dreams
And a vast expanse of immortal feelings
Delivered on a cloud of magic whispers

An end that is a beginning
Where a clock strikes infinity
And an exchange of two hearts
That will last a lifetime beating as one.

Marilyn Holliday

STAR-CROSS'D LOVERS

We walked hand in hand,
she and I,
while the wind felt inside our coats.

Ahead of us, a Star blew across the street
and fetched up against the kerb.
I glanced at it as we passed -

the headline, crumpled
and greasy by then with chip fat,
could not be read.

Meanwhile the sunset went on unnoticed
between the trees,
caught for a moment in the branches.

Where were we heading,
she and I,
with the autumn wind inside our coats?

I forget now.
Past the park I think,
and on towards winter.

Ian Harrison

UNTITLED

Love is a drug, love is all you need,
So the songs say,
But love is a torture and love hurts,
When it goes away.

Love is good and love is hope.
Love is all around.
But love is a burden and love is despair,
When it can't be found.

Love is strength and love is power
And love makes you feel brand new,
And love is lasting and love is forever
For all and not just a few.

Love is for all and love is for one,
And love is both big and small.
Love is freedom and love is tying,
And picks you up when you fall.

Love costs so little but is worth so much.
You can take it wherever you go.
And love is nothing and love is all things
For those of us who know.

Love is good and never bad,
Love is nothing new.
Love is life's only thing,
That no one can take from you.

So save your love and value love's gift.
Don't throw your life away.
Look after love, love will look after you
Forever and a day.

Ivan S Cherry

LOVESCAPE

We have scaled a height greater than Slieve Donard, we two,
You, of the Greenspun cloth, my love, and I, True Blue,
Young ramblers across the tribal divide,
Our togetherness there for all to see,
Nor would we hide.

Our love kindled and grew,
Tender, yet strong as Sperrin heather,
Vibrant as a blaze of golden whins,
Our desire to be together.
We knew it would not be denied,
Though bomb and bullet and threat of baseball bat
Must be defied.

Triumphant, it burst into glorious flame, God-given right -
Nor will the tribal laws of Man put this to flight.
Through the impenetrable, our chink is in the wall.
Greenspun and True Blue, together, we two -
Love conquers all.

Ann Stewart

LOVE

The buzzing bees, a blooming flower,
Makes the world revolve when one's in love.
During every daily waking hour,
The sky seems bluer way up above.

When love is in the air,
Worries just appear to fly away;
Leaving happy thoughts and not a care,
Tempers are cool and never fray.

Of course, we all know love's a phase,
And some days we have to be without.
When you're young, love is the only phrase,
That much is clear, I have no doubt.

But when love is not around
Time ticks by with a dreary groan;
We feel alone - life stands still on the ground.
The buzzing bees become an irritating drone.

And suddenly in a moment of surprise
Along comes love in leaps and bounds
It fills our hearts and opens our eyes
Love is wonderful with all of its sounds.

Nikki Wolfin

AFTERNOON AARDVARK

My love is like an aardvark
That's post-modernist in June,
With mackerel tints soft-painted
Beneath a Domesday moon.
A bungalow awaits us,
On the wall kalashnikovs hang,
So when we tire of loving
We'll go out with a bang.

Joan Woolard

TO CARMAN - DULCIE CARMAN

My Carman
Dear and lovely Carman
I see you pass by
I hold you in my arms
I kiss you and caress you.
Will you be my Valentine?

My Carman
Sweet and lovely Carman
I see you every day
See you in our child,
See your haunting beauty,
Beauty as forever.
Will you be my Valentine?

My Carman
Sweet and lovely Carman
I see you - I see you
As with love and tenderness
We know each other in perfect love.
Will you be my Valentine?

My Carman - Dulcie Carman,
Darling lovely Carman
The light of my youth,
The joy of my middle years,
The peace of my later life,
Be my darling Valentine.

Janet Cavill

YOU GIVE ME EVERYTHING

You give me the moon and stars,
The sun, the clouds, the rain.
You present me with night and day,
You teach me to trust again.

You give me a purpose for living
With hope, with love, with joy.
A chance to change direction
To love myself, not destroy.

Each time you whisper you love me
I see, I feel, I hear
That maybe I am worth loving
And in you, I have nothing to fear.

With your kiss you breathe in new life,
So strong, so deep, so true.
Each stroke of your finger awakens
The desire to be loved by you.

How can you say you do nothing
With love so true, so pure.
When you've opened my heart, like no other,
With you loving me, I'm secure.

Sandie Woodward

ALL GIRLS ARE LOVELY ON A SUMMER'S DAY

All girls are lovely on a summer's day.
I once found fault with one girl's eyes
With one girl's walk, with one girl's thighs
With one who said she loved another
Or one who was always with her mother;
But all girls are lovely on a summer's day.

Peter Rist

TEN YEARS OF LOVE
(To Geoff)

You're always there for me,
Quiet but strong,
I feel secure with you,
We two belong
Together travelling
Along life's path,
We've had our ups and downs,
But still can laugh.

They said it wouldn't work
We knew it would,
We'd both been hurt before
Knew where we stood,
Thought we had love worked out
Both shared our pain,
And then we dared to hope
We'd love again.

We hid our feelings well,
But time moved on,
We found bad memories
Were now all gone,
The love that we both share
So true will last,
Those who we loved before
Are now the past.

We can now celebrate
Ten married years,
Of happy life we've made
And some shared tears,
I love you now as then
I always will,
My sweetest Valentine
I love you still.

Irene Carter

UNTITLED
(To my beloved)

It's many long years since we two were wed
And our love has been sorely tried
But now that we're old it can be said
That our love has never died
The years have been hard and life has been cruel
But our love has kept us together
Our needs are not great but I know that our love
Will be with us forever and ever.

V E Hobbs

MY DEAR

That personality so unique
Your emerald eyes sparkle
And hands of gold

The days of grief
We came through clear
Fighting through fear

Those moments we shared
We must treasure alone
For our relationship to grow.

Bav

SYMBOL

In the shape of things to come
Far between and then some,
Large as life, as full as can be,
Heavenly saints, that's you and me.
The circle is an oval,
The square uneven and broken;
Formed together, can you see
This has made the perfect geometry.
Put together the shapes become,
All we've put into it,
All that we've done.
Made from all the things we have,
Physical and emotional
A symbol of love.

Adam Davis

SEASONS OF LOVE

Spring stirs the heart,
Love is in the air,
Together, never to part,
For one another we care,
Passionate and new;
Love is you.

Summer bonds our love,
Lazy days and romance,
Forever, we will be,
So happy, I could dance,
Romantic and true;
Love is you.

Autumn leaves us burning,
Consumed with love so strong,
Together, longing and yearning,
We play our special song,
One but two;
Love is you.

Winter sees a promise,
Made amongst the Christmas cheer,
Forever, sealed with a kiss,
For one held so dear,
A future filled with happiness,
May all our dreams come true,
A lifetime together,
I love you.

Amanda S Holland

So You Thought He Forgot!

Sat cross-legged . . . waiting
The card from him
The card you're anticipating
        . . . better come

For a moment you're thinking
What if he forgot
You disregard the thought
Without even blinking
        . . . he wouldn't forget

The rattle of the letter box
Has you on all fours
Peering like a curious fox
Through the metal flap
        . . . any minute now!

A fistful of letters fall
Dull thud as they hit the floor
Only bills, nothing more
One thought
        . . . I hate him

Starting to cry
A tear touching your eye
A straggler floats through the door
Red envelope hits the floor
        . . . what's this?

You know he loves you
You know he cares
Clamber to the phone, jumping stairs
Just to say to him
        . . . I really love you!

Jenny Nicol

SHE

Look at those eyes with the twinkling smile,
could they really hide vanity and guile.
And the innocent toss of her shining hair,
her laugh and the clothing, does she really not care.
Do those lips hide a darker side,
and if I mention love would she laughingly deride.
Here she comes now, I shall lay my soul bare,
but she passes by, because I'm lost, and did not dare.

Joe Waterman

FROM THE HEART

There is so much love in my heart, in so many different ways,
So where can the poetry start to the people that fill my days.
My husband, with eyes so blue, you wrap me in warm embrace,
I would be nowhere without you, your love shines out from your face.
Two special children who I adore, and who need me, oh, so much,
I could never love you more, as I give you a mother's touch.
Dad, you always make me smile, your thoughts you bury deep,
But you are with me all the while, with the memories that I keep.
Dear Mum, in Heaven's restful sky, so far away, so near,
There hasn't been a day gone by, that I haven't wished you here.
Families bless, for good or bad, the torch will forever shine,
Whether you make me happy or sad, I care, for you're always mine.
Loving friends, special times with you, fill us with such pleasure,
And all the little things you do, brings happiness you can't measure.
A special hug to those of you, who feel in any pain,
When you feel all sad and blue, may the sunshine melt your rain.
So to everyone, young or old, and creatures great and small,
Let the world be a happy place, with love for one and all.

Patricia Kelly

LOVE IS . . .

Love is heavenly, love is bliss
Love is waking to your kiss.

Love is silent, love is true
Love is snuggling next to you.

Love is sharing, love is strong
Love is caring in a wrong.

Love is helping, love is you
Love is coping when I'm blue.

Love is perfect, love is free
Love is binding you to me.

Love is heavenly, love is bliss
Love is waking to your kiss.

Betty Lightfoot

HEART-SHAPED MANUAL

My mother gave me life and
My wife gave my sons life

No, no, let's be serious

Real love cannot be bought,
We show our love in many ways,
Often it starts from a caring thought

Even words spoken on St Valentine's
Day, a loving cuddle or kiss
Especially when love makes you
Speechless.

Buying your lover a loving card
Need never be hard.

Just look around, if you're short
Of money, instead send a homemade
St Valentine's card to your honey.

Some thin scrap card, scissors,
A pen or pencil, even finish
Off the front, with a heart
Shaped stencil.

To you. It's cost you little
Except precious time
Given you much pleasure showing
Off your artistic measure.

A final touch to the inside
Reminding her your love has never died.

And think, this time, you! Have
The final word, written in rhyme.

Peter James-Young

TOO LATE

True love, is it stuff of dreams?
That has no place in nature's schemes,
I've searched for it to no avail,
A becalmed ship without a sail.
Where is the woman of my dreams?
No Miss Right for me it seems,
I've longed for her for these past years
My loneliness brought private tears.
Young men, do not trust to fate
I did, now it seems too late.

Richard F Youngs

THE CHRISTMAS CRACKER

An admiring glance said it all,
She was his Christmas cracker that was having a ball,
He watched her smile and watched her dance,
Until he was sent into a strange sort of trance.

He dreamed first of lust, then love ever more
And maybe a few children, possibly four,
A sudden blush came over his face,
As their eyes clashed together,
His heart began to race.

Perhaps she was dreaming fairy tales too,
And looking for that Christmas cracker,
To make our dreams come true.

Tony Beaven

YOU ARE EVERYTHING

You are the moon and stars to me
The waves that sparkle on the sea
You are the sun that warms the earth
The miracle of every birth
You are the flowers, jewel bright
The sweet scent of a summer's night
You are the smile on a baby's face
A fond remembered, special place
You are a bird's soft feathered wings
The epitome of lovely things
You are my world, my heaven too,
All pleasure in my life is you.

Barbara L Jones

VIBRANT LOVE

'Love is dead', I've heard some say,
But no! Love never dies.
My heart still warms with glowing love
Though now my dear in cold grave lies.
Love never dies!

Love lives on in heaven and earth,
In every bird that sings.
When arms reach out in fond embrace,
And thoughts fly out on searching wings,
Love ever springs.

Yes! Love endures bright and warm,
Reaches out to us all,
Transcends the hatred of this world,
Lightens the gloom of death's dark pall;
Love conquers all!

Evelyn Balmain

TOUCH

I can touch pearls, polo ponies,
Chauffeurs and champagne
But not your face, or your green eyes,
My world you disdain
Your hatred, my love, yet as magnets
We're drawn
Boxing shadows will merge one
Subliminal dawn
In clouded silk sheets I will touch,
You'll be mine
Love's war will be over, touched by
Morning's light.

Amelia Nixon

THAT WONDROUS FEELING

The story of *love* is ageless
It has been known, since the world began,
Originally, a biblical tale of *Adam* and *Eve*
And termed '*love*' by *woman* and *man*.

Our first *love* usually takes shape
In the puberty of youth,
We begin to carry a torch, in our hearts
And seldom listen to the truth.

Love can be tender - *love* can be oh, so cruel
A jealous mistress with a vicious tongue,
Love can be musical, a sweet operatic aria
A magic melody pleading to be sung.

Love can be an aphrodisiac
To soothe the savage breast,
But beware, it can also be prejudicial
To the detriment of all the rest.

The word *love* is often misapplied
It has been quoted to describe '*Mass Hysteria*',
To *leaders, dictators, film* and *pop stars*
Which can be degrading, and somewhat inferior.

Nevertheless, *true love* is an apex - a pinnacle
Which mere words cannot fully describe,
A wondrous feeling, of contentment, worry, caring and sharing
A wondrous feeling, that only *lovers* feel deep inside.

Paul Gold

LOVE

What is love?
A hug, a kiss
Or just someone who cares?

A word that spans all ages
All cultures and all creeds
The little things that mean so much
To those we hold most dear.

A bunch of flowers, a box of chocs
Or maybe some small present
But the best of all is to hear you say
'I love you', again and again.

Mary A Slater

Love Maketh Love

All encompassing warmth, with passion,
Soft and gentle like a feathered down,
Proof of giving, seldom taking,
Yet taken for granted all around.

A heart that is troubled,
Is soon enlightened,
With all the attributes of this love,
Sacrifice, with tender feelings,
And oft is only known, as love.

Don't take for granted,
This profound emotion,
Give it back and thriceley so,
Treasure it with soul endearing,
And watch it slowly, slowly, grow.

Amelia Simms

TRADITION

The sculpture of a golden rose
Pearled with morning dew
Glistening, in the early sun
This I give to you.

The blanket of a bluebell wood
With shaft of light anew,
The Dresden of a million bells
I offer these to you.

The virgin white of lily
I'll place into your hand,
And then I'll seal your vows to me
With golden of a band.

I'll give you life within you
I'll hold your hand in pain,
And as we melt again as one
I'll give you life again.

I'll love you as each flower of life
Has never loved before,
I'll love you more than love itself
And then I'll love you more.

K Dove

SOPHIE

Lovely Sophie you are the air I breathe, the stuff of poetry,
subject of sonnets and the vision of all my dreams.
I'm intoxicated by the perfume of your lustrous hair cascading
around shoulders soft and ivory.
A strand of shimmering gold breaks free partially concealing
your lovely face and parted red lips sweet as honey.
I bless the day we met a vision of loveliness wearing a rose
coloured organza dress floating around like the petals of a
giant hibiscus trying to be pollinated by a reluctant bee.
It is not possible to erase you from my mind and my aching
heart cries out in protest against the punishment it is
receiving from perpetual yearning for you lovely Sophie.

Oh Lover, tell me I am beautiful and your love is sincere,
reassure me nothing will wither my body or the roses in my lips,
and nothing will tarnish the gold of my hair, even when I grow
old I shall always be beautiful in your eyes.

Lovely Sophie I shall always delight in telling you of my love,
I love you in spirit, I love you in truth, my love for you will
never waver.
Fear not my one and only Love, I will love you forever.

Dorothy F White

Come Sit Beside Me

Come here and sit beside me Pet.
Please show me that you care
Then I will fetch a gentle brush
To smooth your shining hair.
And I will whisper secrets
If you promise not to tell.
I'm sure you keep your promises,
I know you very well.
You never say you love me
But if I go you're sad,
Then I come back, no need for words
It's obvious you're glad.
So I will sit alongside you
And show you how much *I* care
And in a way my four-pawed friend
We'll be a perfect pair.

June Marshall

MY VALENTINE

I send to you this gift of love
And hope it will convey
How very much you mean to me
How you help from day to day
To make my world seem brighter
My sorrows fade from sight
You help me face each brand new day
And fill my dreams at night
Soon we shall be together
You've promised to be mine
But until then my dearest
Please accept this Valentine.

Lydia Barnett

INFORMATION

We hope you have enjoyed reading this book - and that you will continue to enjoy it in the coming years.

If you like reading and writing poetry drop us a line, or give us a call, and we'll send you a free information pack.

Write to :-
Poetry Now Information
1-2 Wainman Road
Woodston
Peterborough
PE2 7BU
(01733) 230746